Early SCIENCE Encyclopedias

WEATHER

by A. W. Buckey

Early Encyclopedias

An Imprint of Abdo Reference

abdobooks.com

abdobooks.com

Published by Abdo Reference, a division of ABDO, PO Box 398166, Minneapolis, Minnesota 55439.

Printed in China.
052024
092024

THIS BOOK CONTAINS RECYCLED MATERIALS

Editor: Marie Pearson
Series Designers: Candice Keimig, Joshua Olson
Production Designer: Joshua Olson

Library of Congress Control Number: 2023949416

Publisher's Cataloging-in-Publication Data

Names: Buckey, A. W., author.
Title: Weather / by A. W. Buckey
Description: Minneapolis, Minnesota: Abdo Reference, 2025 | Series: Early science encyclopedias | Includes online resources and index.
Identifiers: ISBN 9781098294298 (lib. bdg.) | ISBN 9798384913566 (ebook)
Subjects: LCSH: Weather--Juvenile literature. | Meteorology--Juvenile literature. | Earth sciences--Juvenile literature. | Climate--Juvenile literature. | Science--Juvenile literature. | Encyclopedias and dictionaries--Juvenile literature.
Classification: DDC 551.6--dc23

CONTENTS

Introduction **4**

Clouds 6
Rain 14
Sleet 22
Hail 30
Snow 38
Fog 46
Dew and Frost 54
Thunder and Lightning 62
Hurricanes 70
Tornadoes 80
Droughts 90
Wildfires 98
Dust Storms 108
Heat Waves 116
Climate Change and Weather 124

Glossary **126**
To Learn More **127**
Index **127**
Photo Credits **128**

It is always raining somewhere on Earth.

Weather

Every day on Earth is different. Sometimes it is hot and sunny outside. Other times, the sky is full of rain. Some parts of the world are drier or colder than others.

Changing Weather

Every place on Earth has changes in heat, air movement, and water. These changes happen in the atmosphere, the air that surrounds Earth. They are called weather. Some weather can be dangerous. But weather helps life on Earth grow.

The atmosphere gets thinner farther away from Earth.

What Are Clouds?

Clouds are in the atmosphere. They are made of water. Water can come in many forms. Frozen water is a solid called ice. The water in oceans is liquid water. Clouds can be made of ice or liquid water.

Clouds are clusters of water.

Despite how fluffy clouds can look, they are not solid but are made mostly of air.

Tiny Drops

The drops of water that form clouds are very small. They are so small that they do not fall to the ground. Instead, wind pushes them up in the sky.

Cloud Color

Clouds often look white against the blue sky. This is because sunlight hits air and water differently.

The appearance of clouds is sometimes a sign that a change in weather is coming.

Types of Clouds

There are many types of clouds. They differ in shape and size. They form at different heights in the atmosphere. Clouds can be high, medium, or low.

FUN FACT!

The exhaust from airplanes can make clouds. These clouds are called contrails.

High Clouds

High clouds are above 20,000 feet (6,100 m) from the ground. These clouds have *cirr* in their names. Their look depends on the type and amount of water. For example, the cirrus cloud is thin and wispy. It is usually made of ice crystals. This is because the air is colder higher in the atmosphere.

Cirrus **is Latin for "a lock of hair."**

Medium Clouds

Medium clouds form between 6,500 and 20,000 feet (2,000 and 6,100 m). These clouds have *alto* in their names. The altostratus cloud is long and flat. It can be a sign warm air is coming.

Altostratus clouds can get thick enough to make the Sun seem dim.

Low Clouds

Low clouds form between the ground and 6,500 feet (2,000 m). Some low clouds, such as stratus clouds, are wide and make the sky gray. Others are fluffy such as cumulus clouds.

Strong wind flattens out the top of a cumulonimbus cloud.

Making Rain

Sometimes the water drops in clouds get bigger and heavier. The wind can't keep them in the air. They fall from the sky as rain, snow, or other forms.

Rain Clouds

Not all clouds make rain or snow. The ones that do have *nimb* in their names. For example, a cumulonimbus cloud stretches from the low to the high atmosphere. Cumulonimbus clouds make storms.

Cloud Types

There are many types of clouds. They come in a variety of shapes.

What Is Rain?

Rain is liquid water that falls from the sky. Rain comes from clouds filled with water droplets. The droplets bump into each other and grow. When they are heavy enough, they fall from the cloud. A normal raindrop is about the thickness of a nickel.

Drizzle

Very small raindrops are called drizzle. They are smaller than 0.02 inches (0.5 mm).

Plants use rainwater to grow.

Types of Rainfall

Rainfall comes in a few types. They are relief rainfall, convective rainfall, and frontal rainfall. They all form in different ways.

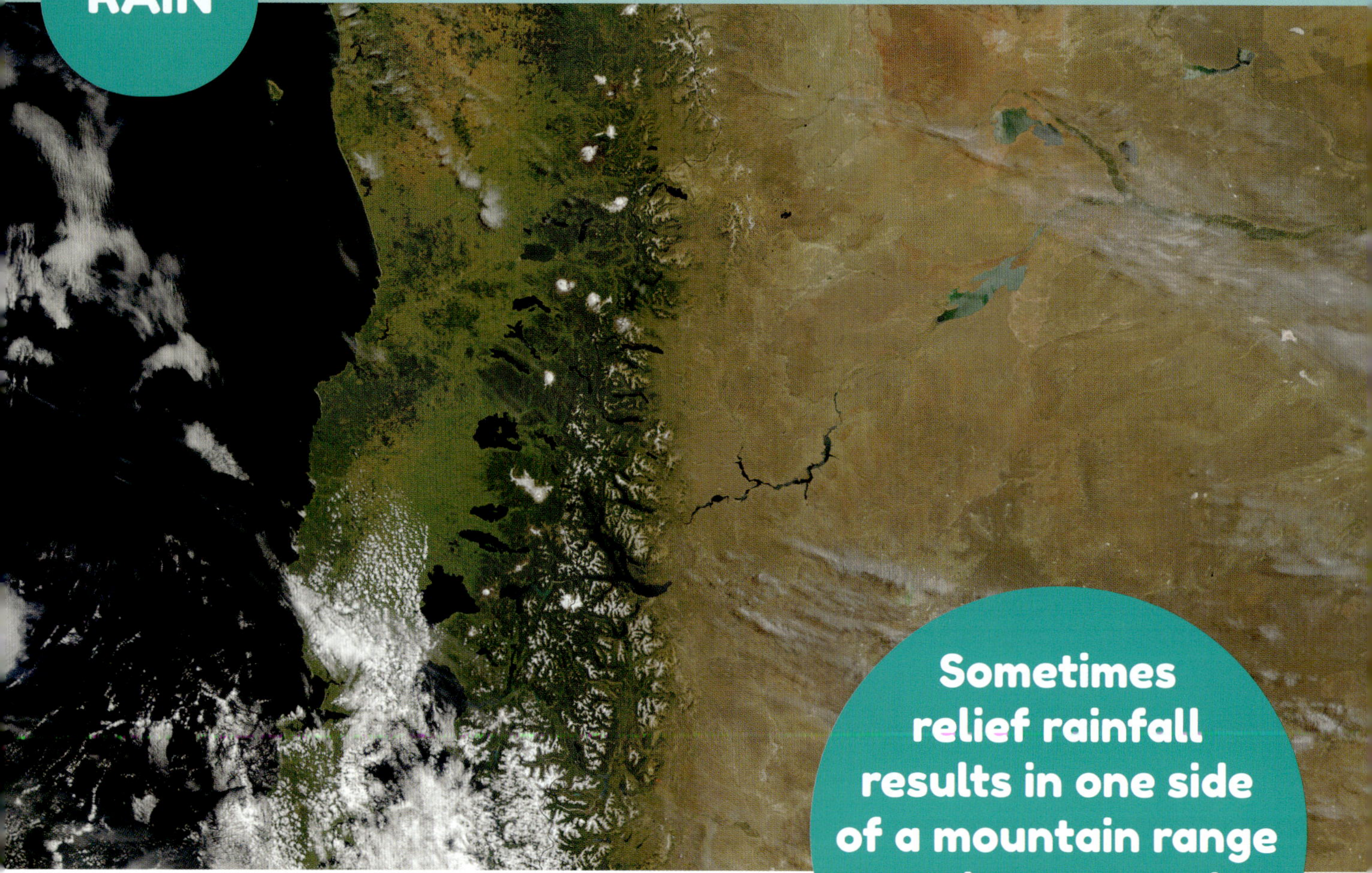

Sometimes relief rainfall results in one side of a mountain range getting more rain than the other side.

Relief Rainfall

Relief rainfall forms over hills and mountains. As air travels up the slopes, it cools. The cooling air turns vapor into raindrops. The water condenses, or comes together. Because of the cooler air, mountains get more rain than nearby low areas.

Convective Rainfall

Convective rainfall happens in hot, moist areas. When the ground gets hotter, it warms the air. The warm air rises and cools. Raindrops condense and fall.

Frontal Rainfall

Frontal rainfall happens when warm air and cold air meet. The cold air pushes the warm air upward. The warm air cools, clouds form, and rain falls.

Convective rainfall brings lots of rain to rainforests.

Plants release water in the form of water vapor.

The Water Cycle

Rain is part of the water cycle. The water cycle is the way water travels between the ground and sky. Rain goes into the ground or into lakes and rivers. Plants can use the water to grow. The plants release water back into the air.

Water Cycle in the Air

Water also evaporates from the ground or a body of water. It turns into water vapor. It rises into the air to form clouds. The clouds make rain. The cycle goes on.

The Water Cycle

Water is always moving. This helps living things get the water they need to live.

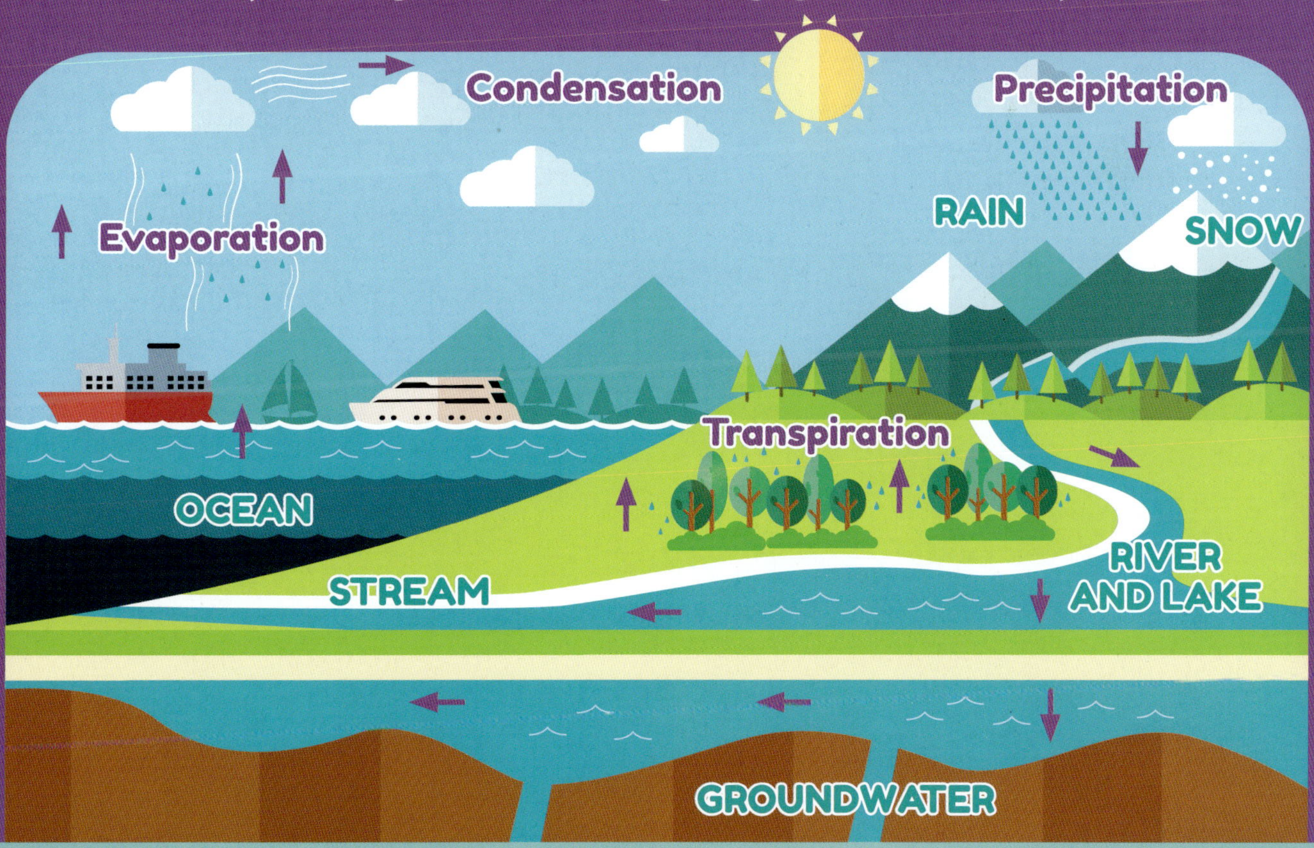

Effects of Rain

Plants and animals need rain to live. Humans do too. Rain fills lakes and rivers. These are major water sources for living things.

Umbrellas and waterproof clothing can keep people dry when it rains.

Floods are the most common natural disaster on Earth.

Atmospheric Rivers

Large amounts of water evaporate from tropical areas. Earth has winds that push this water vapor toward the poles. The poles are the bottom and top parts of Earth. The movement of this vapor forms atmospheric rivers. These rivers can cause huge rainstorms and floods. But they also carry needed rain.

FUN FACT!

The rainiest place on Earth is Mount Waialeale in Hawaii. It gets 38 feet (12 m) of rain a year.

Sleet Versus Freezing Rain

Sleet and freezing rain both form when snow melts as it falls. But freezing rain falls as liquid water. It freezes when it hits a cold surface. Sleet turns back into ice before it hits the ground.

Freezing rain can form icicles when it hits cold objects.

Precipitation Conditions

The layers of warm and cold air determine what type of precipitation falls.

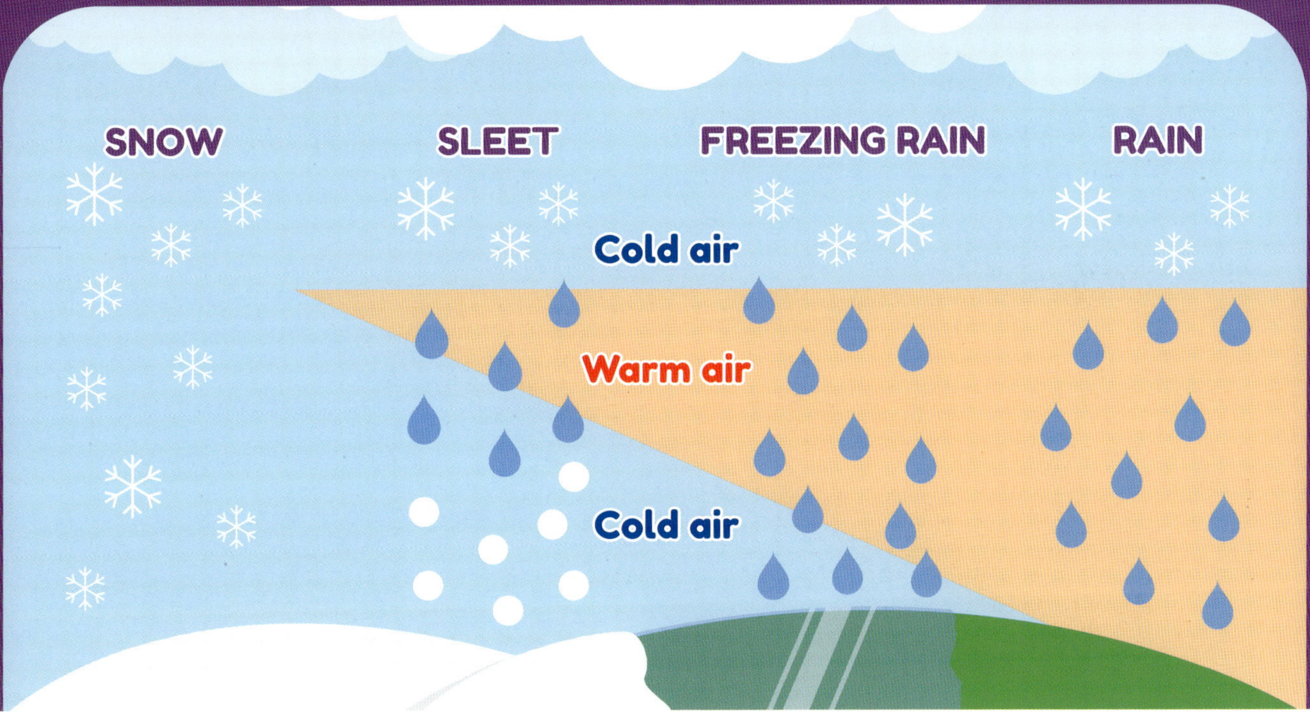

Warm Fronts

Sleet usually happens north of a warm front. A warm front is a place where warm air pushes above cold air. This action forms clouds.

FUN FACT!

Some people use the word *sleet* to mean any mix of snow and rain.

In the United Kingdom, sleet is called ice pellets.

Where Sleet Happens

In the United States, sleet is most common in the winter. Some air is likely to be below freezing. Sleet tends to be heaviest in the Southeast. This area often has warm weather, even in winter. A mix of different air temperatures there is likely.

Effects of Sleet

Sleet can be dangerous. Ice pellets can cause damage as they fall from the sky. Sleet can build up on a roof. This can cause leaks.

Record Sleet

In 2015 the city of Chicago, Illinois, got 1.9 inches (4.8 cm) of sleet in a day. That was a record amount.

Discoloration or mold are signs that a house's roof is leaking.

Slippery Roads

One of sleet's biggest dangers is that it makes the ground slippery. Sleet coats roads with ice. The ice can make roads slick and unsafe for driving.

Black ice is a thin layer of ice on roads. It can be hard for drivers to see black ice.

Coldest Roads

The ground stays warmer than the air in winter. Bridges and elevated roads are more exposed to the weather. Ice appears on them more quickly than on other sections of road. That can make them more slippery.

Hail can be cloudy or clear depending on how it is formed.

What Is Hail?

Like sleet, hail is ice pellets. But hail is bigger than sleet. An ice pellet more than 0.2 inches (5 mm) wide is called hail. This is a little smaller than the size of a pea.

Making Hail

Hail and sleet form in different ways. Hail forms inside thunderstorms. Rain from inside a thunderstorm is swept upward. There, it freezes together into ice pellets. Hail usually comes from cumulonimbus clouds.

Hail Growth

Hail grows bigger as it travels through a cloud.

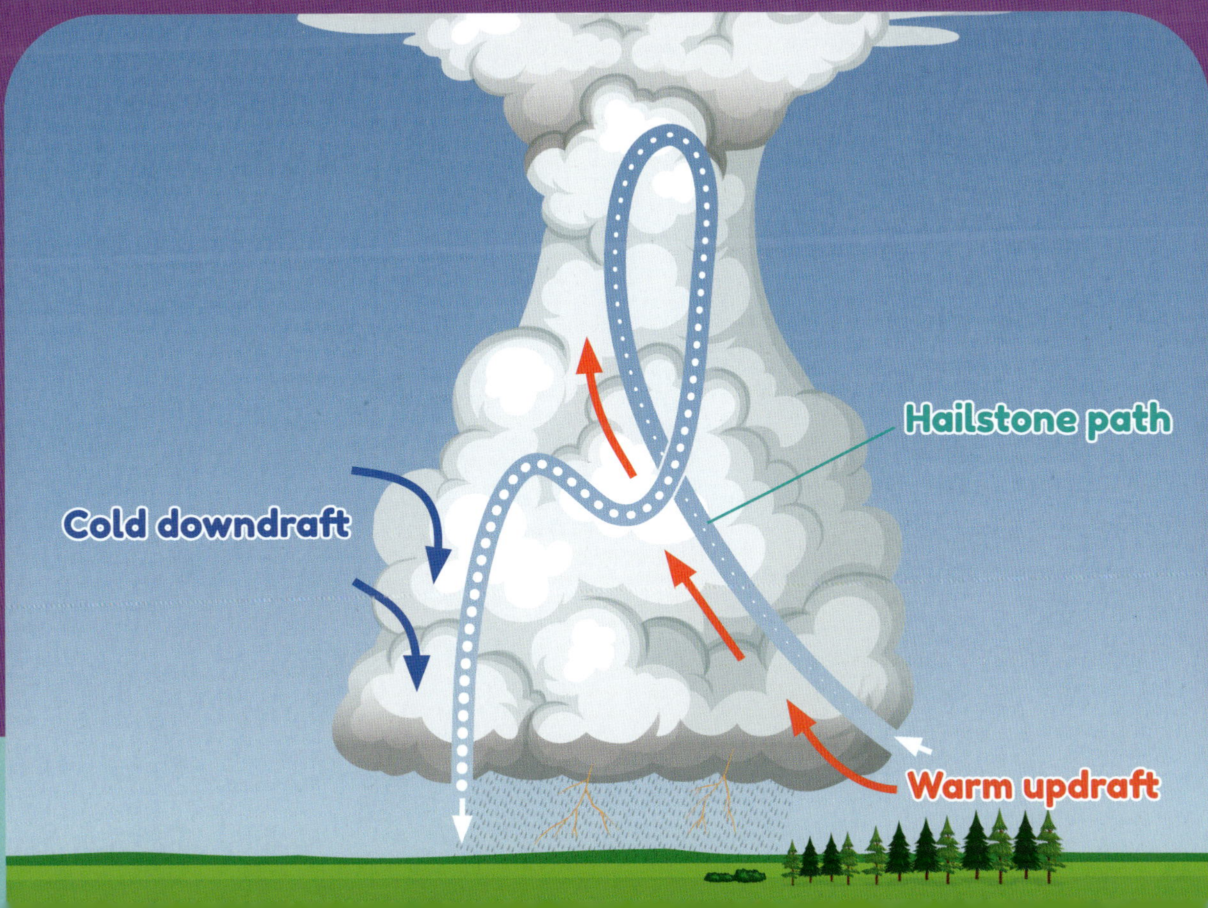

Where Hail Is Found

In the United States, hail happens most often in Nebraska, Colorado, and Wyoming. Italy, China, India, Russia, central Africa, and southern South America are other places that get a lot of hail.

Sometimes the sky gets green before a hailstorm or thunderstorm. Researchers are still trying to figure out why this happens.

Hail can fall on days with temperatures of 80 degrees Fahrenheit (27°C) or higher.

Timing

Hail is more likely to fall in summer than in winter. Hail forms when temperatures are warm enough for thunderstorms. Hailstorms are most likely to happen in the afternoon. They usually last about 15 minutes.

Hail Alley

The place where Nebraska, Wyoming, and Colorado meet is called Hail Alley. It has about seven to nine days with hail each year.

The air is usually warm enough that hail begins to melt before it even hits the ground.

Freezing

Hail forms when water in the air reaches very high into the atmosphere. There, temperatures are cold. The water freezes into hail. Then it falls to the ground.

Sizes of Hail

The size of hail depends on the updraft that makes it. An updraft is the wind that sweeps water into the upper atmosphere. When the updraft is stronger, the rain has more time to stick together and freeze. This forms bigger hail.

FUN FACT!

The heaviest piece of hail ever measured weighed more than 2.2 pounds (1 kg).

Larger hail falls faster than smaller hail.

Measuring Hail

There is a system for measuring hail. It matches each size of hail to a common object. The National Weather Service lists 14 hail sizes. The smallest is pea size. The largest is grapefruit size. Most hailstorms have a mix of different sizes.

Hail Sizes

Everyday items that people are familiar with help others picture the size of hail.

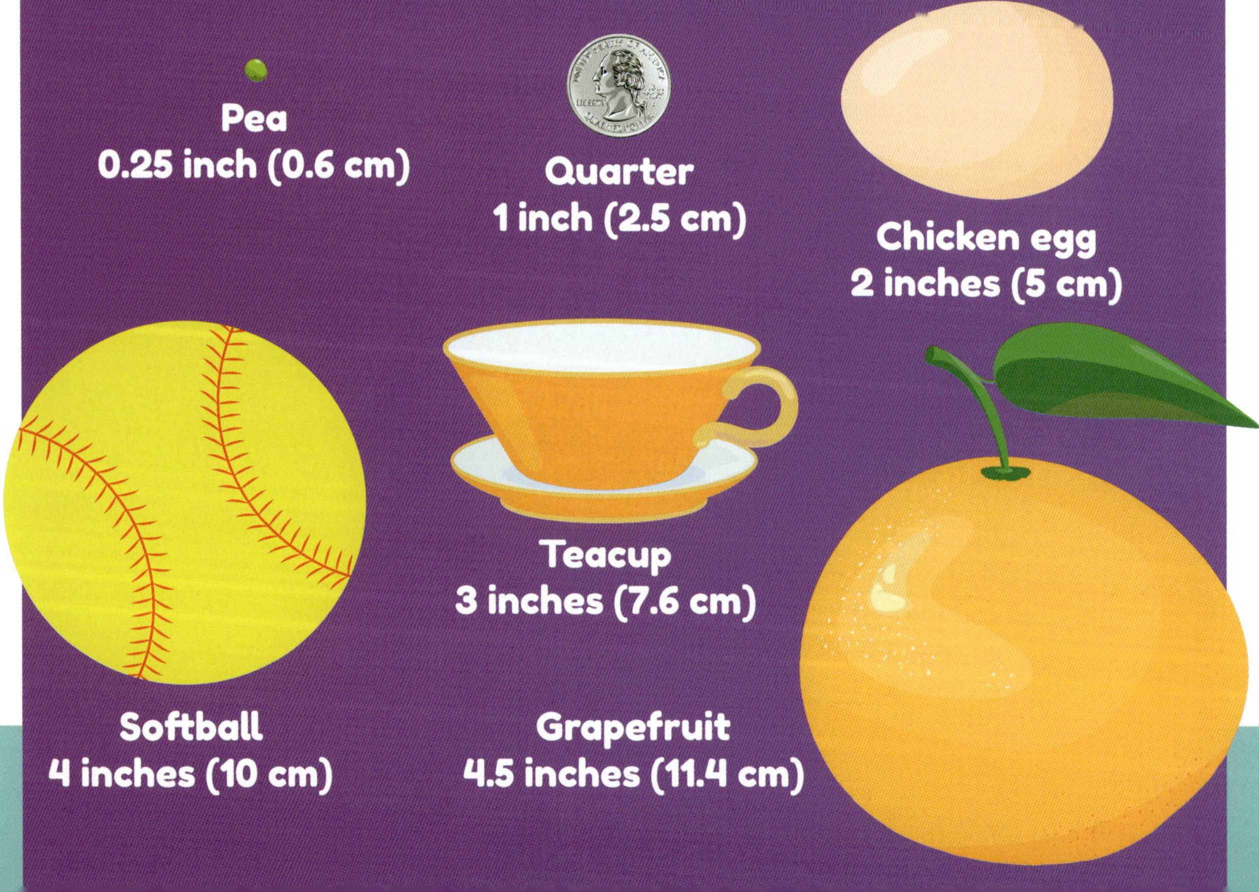

Hail can smash car windshields.

Effects of Hail

Hail can be dangerous. It can damage buildings and plants when it hits them. Hail can also cause power outages. Large hail can be deadly when it hits people or animals. It is best to stay indoors during a hailstorm.

When it is cold enough outside, snow stays frozen on the ground.

What Is Snow?

Snow is frozen water that falls from clouds. Snow forms when the atmosphere temperature is below freezing. The water inside clouds freezes onto tiny particles. These particles can be pieces of dust or pollen in the sky.

Adding Ice

The frozen water makes a six-sided ice crystal called a snowflake. More water freezes onto the sides of this six-sided shape. The freezing water creates the spiny shapes on the sides of the flakes.

Snowflake Growth

Snowflakes grow as more ice is added to them.

SNOW

Falling

When enough ice freezes and the snowflake becomes heavy, it falls. Each snowflake forms in slightly different conditions. This means each snowflake's shape is a little different.

Snowflakes are highly symmetrical. Rotating them around their center can leave them looking the same as before the rotation.

Types of Snowfall

There are different types of snowfall. Flurries happen when snow falls lightly. They do not usually leave snow on the ground. A snow shower can be light or heavy. It will often leave snow on the ground. A snow squall is a short and intense storm. It usually lasts an hour or less.

Blizzards can quickly cover animals and objects in snow.

Blizzards

The strongest snowstorms are called blizzards. A blizzard is a storm with falling and blowing snow. Blizzard winds are more than 35 miles per hour (56 kmh).

Where Snow Happens

Snow is most likely in winter, when the weather is cold. Snow can form even in Earth's coldest temperatures. Snow can also fall in high places, such as mountaintops, in warm regions. This is because high elevations are colder than low areas.

Wet snow is easier than dry snow to mold into shapes such as snow people.

FUN FACT!

At any time, about 23 percent of the world is covered in snow.

Effects of Snowfall

Layers of snow on the ground are called snowpack. Snowpack is a source of water. But it can be dangerous. Large amounts of snowpack sliding down mountains are called avalanches. They can quickly cover and trap people.

Blizzards can happen without any falling snow. Wind kicks up snow already on the ground, making it hard to see.

Travel

Snow can make it hard to travel. For example, blizzards can create whiteouts. During a whiteout, it becomes very hard to see because of blowing snow.

To count as fog, a cloud must limit visibility to less than 3,280 feet (1,000 m) ahead.

What Is Fog?

Fog is a cloud that reaches the ground. Fog happens in humid weather. Humid air has a lot of moisture.

Particles

Fog happens when water condenses around particles in the air. Particles are very small. They can be dust, salt, and other small bits. Condensation happens when there is a lot of moisture in the air. Condensation is also more likely when air cools.

Mist

Water vapor too light to be fog is called mist. Mist is easier to see through than fog.

Water vapor is invisible, so fog only happens when water becomes liquid in the air.

Types of Fog

There are many types of fog. Advection fog happens when warm air flows over a cold place. Ground fog happens when the ground loses heat. This cools the air near the surface. Upslope fog comes from air that travels up a mountain. The air cools as it moves upward.

Fog can collect in valleys between mountains.

Steam fog occurs over water that is warmer than the air above it.

More Types

Steam fog forms when water vapor meets colder air. Frontal fog happens near a front, where warm and cold air mix. Ice fog is fog made of ice crystals. Human activities can cause ice fog. For example, exhaust from cars and airplanes gives off water vapor. In very cold temperatures, this can create ice fog.

Effects of Fog

Fog blocks some heat from the Sun. Fog can make it hard to see. It can be hard to drive a car or steer a ship through fog. Plants and animals in deserts sometimes get water from fog.

Slowing down and using low-beam headlights can help keep drivers safe in foggy conditions.

Pollution

Fog also attaches to harmful particles such as soot and smoke. This is called smog. The name comes from a mix of smoke and fog. It is a type of air pollution. Smog in the air makes it harder to breathe and see.

Dew often forms on blades of grass in lawns.

What Is Dew?

Dew is condensed moisture. It forms on the ground or on plants. Cooling temperatures cause vapor near the ground to turn to liquid water. This water can come from the air or the ground.

Dew Point

The temperature at which dew forms is called the dew point. The dew point is higher with a lot of moisture in the air. It is lower with less moisture.

Humid and Dry

On days with a high dew point, the air feels humid. When there is a low dew point, the air feels dry.

Dew Point

The more moisture is in the air, the more uncomfortable the air feels, and a higher temperature is needed for dew to form.

Dew Point	How the Humidity Feels Outside
Higher than 80 degrees Fahrenheit (27°C)	Severely oppressive
75–80 degrees Fahrenheit (24–27°C)	Fairly oppressive
70–74 degrees Fahrenheit (21–23°C)	Quite uncomfortable
65–69 degrees Fahrenheit (18–21°C)	Somewhat uncomfortable
60–64 degrees Fahrenheit (16–18°C)	Okay for most
55–59 degrees Fahrenheit (13–15°C)	Comfortable
50–54 degrees Fahrenheit (10–12°C)	Very comfortable
49 degrees Fahrenheit (9°C) or lower	A bit dry

When Dew Happens

Dew usually forms at night. Temperatures get cooler at night. This means early mornings are often dewy.

Dew forms best during nights with little wind.

The web-footed gecko lives in the desert, where water can be hard to find.

Effects of Dew

Dew helps keeps soil moist. It keeps water in the ground from evaporating. Dew helps plants stay cool in hot weather. Some plants take in dew from their leaves. Animals such as squirrels can drink dew. The web-footed gecko drinks dew that collects on its eyes.

What Is Frost?

Frost is like frozen dew. It forms on the ground and on plants. But frost is a thin layer of ice instead of liquid water.

Types of Frost

There are a few types of frost. Radiation frost is also called hoarfrost. This frost forms when water in the air meets objects that are very cold. It freezes onto the objects.

FUN FACT!

People once thought that hoarfrost on May 1 was a sign of good crops to come.

The word *hoar* means "graying with age." Hoarfrost is called that because it looks like the hair of a gray beard.

Advection and Window Frost

Advection frost forms when cold air blows across objects. It makes spikes of ice. Window frost forms on glass. It happens when outside air is cold and inside moisture touches the glass.

Advection frost, *left*, and window frost, *right*

Young plants are usually more vulnerable to frost than mature plants.

Effects of Frost

Sometimes frost settles on farm crops. This frost can stop plants from growing. The cold and ice dry out and damage the plants. This is sometimes called a killing frost.

Large cities can have a higher risk of thunderstorms than nearby areas. This may be because cities are hotter and have more pollution.

What Is Lightning?

All matter is made of atoms. Atoms have parts called electrons. Sometimes electrons move from atom to atom. This movement of energy is called electricity. Lightning is a type of electricity.

Traveling Electrons

Lightning happens when electricity sparks in the air. Electrons build up in part of a cloud. This causes an electric charge. The electrons travel to the ground, to another spot in the air, or to another cloud. The electricity flashes across the sky in lightning bolts.

Lightning from cloud to cloud or cloud to air is called a cloud flash.

What Is Thunder?

Lightning releases heat as it travels. This heat makes the air expand quickly. The quickly spreading air creates a shock wave. The sound of this shock wave is called thunder.

FUN FACT!

The air around a lightning bolt can get hotter than the Sun's surface.

Because lightning is so hot, it can burn objects it hits, such as trees.

There are about 20 million cloud-to-ground lightning flashes in the lower 48 US states each year.

Different Sounds

Thunder sounds different when close or far. Close to a lightning bolt, thunder sounds like a loud tearing. A little farther, it sounds like a crack. And farther than that, it sounds low and rumbling.

THUNDER AND LIGHTNING

A person has just a one in 1.2 million chance of getting struck by lightning.

How They Go Together

Thunder comes from lightning. It cannot exist without it. Thunder always comes after lightning. This is because light travels faster than sound. A lightning bolt appears in the sky first. Then the shock wave from the heat makes its noise.

Distance

It is possible to hear thunder about 10 miles (16 km) away from lightning. However, lightning can be visible for up to 200 miles (320 m). So it is possible to see lightning and not hear thunder.

Some buildings have lightning rods. When lightning strikes, it hits the rods, which send the energy safely to the ground.

Thunderstorm Conditions

Lightning and thunder usually come with rain. This is because water in a cloud helps form an electric charge. Rainfall alongside lightning and thunder is called a thunderstorm. Some thunderstorms are small. They last up to an hour. Bigger storms can last many hours.

Rain clouds are dark. There is so much water that it blocks sunlight.

Storm chasers follow severe weather such as thunderstorms to monitor them and help keep others safe.

Effects

Lightning can be very dangerous. The electricity from a lightning strike can hurt or kill people. People should stay out of open areas during thunderstorms.

Hurricanes can be seen from space.

What Is a Hurricane?

A hurricane is a type of strong storm. It is a kind of tropical cyclone. Tropical cyclones form when there is a low-pressure system above the warm ocean. When air is at low pressure, wind is drawn toward it.

Making a Hurricane

The warm ocean water travels into the air. Then warm air and moisture rise to make clouds. Thunderstorms begin to form. At the same time, circling winds begin to pick up speed. These fast, spiraling winds travel across the ocean. When the wind reaches a speed of 74 miles per hour (119 kmh), the storm is a hurricane.

Hurricanes bring very strong winds that can damage plants and human-made structures.

Strong winds and storm surges can destroy coastal buildings.

Effects of Hurricanes

A hurricane is one of the most dangerous types of weather. When a hurricane hits land, it can cause a lot of damage. The wind causes ocean waves to rise above normal levels. This is called a storm surge. A storm surge can stretch across hundreds of miles of shoreline.

Other Damage

The wind and flooding can destroy roads and buildings. Flooding can tear away land on the coast. Hurricanes may also pollute the water. They dump ocean water into fresh water.

Storm surges can carry boats inland and leave them stranded when the storm ends.

What Is a Tornado?

A tornado comes from a thunderstorm. Thunderstorms have quickly moving air. Warm air rises, and cool air falls. The upward movement of air is called an updraft.

Tornadoes are visible only if moisture, dust, and debris get trapped in them.

Tornadoes can come from rotating thunderstorms called supercells.

Making a Tornado

Sometimes, an updraft turns around. It stops moving upward. Instead, the air spins and rotates out from the cloud. This is a funnel cloud. When the spinning air reaches to the ground, it is a tornado. The tornado travels with the thunderstorm.

About 1,200 tornadoes hit the United States each year, damaging neighborhoods and other places.

Where Tornadoes Are Found

Tornadoes are most common in the middle latitudes of Earth. These areas reach between the tropics and the Arctic and Antarctic Circles. Warm air and cold air come together in these places. There are more tornadoes in the United States than in any other country. The United States also has the world's strongest tornadoes.

Tornado Alley

US tornadoes are most common in a region of land from Texas to the upper Midwest. This area is called Tornado Alley. Dry air mixes with warm, moist air from the Gulf of Mexico. The mixture causes rotation.

Tornado Alley Map

Not everyone agrees on which states are included in Tornado Alley. This map shows one common suggestion.

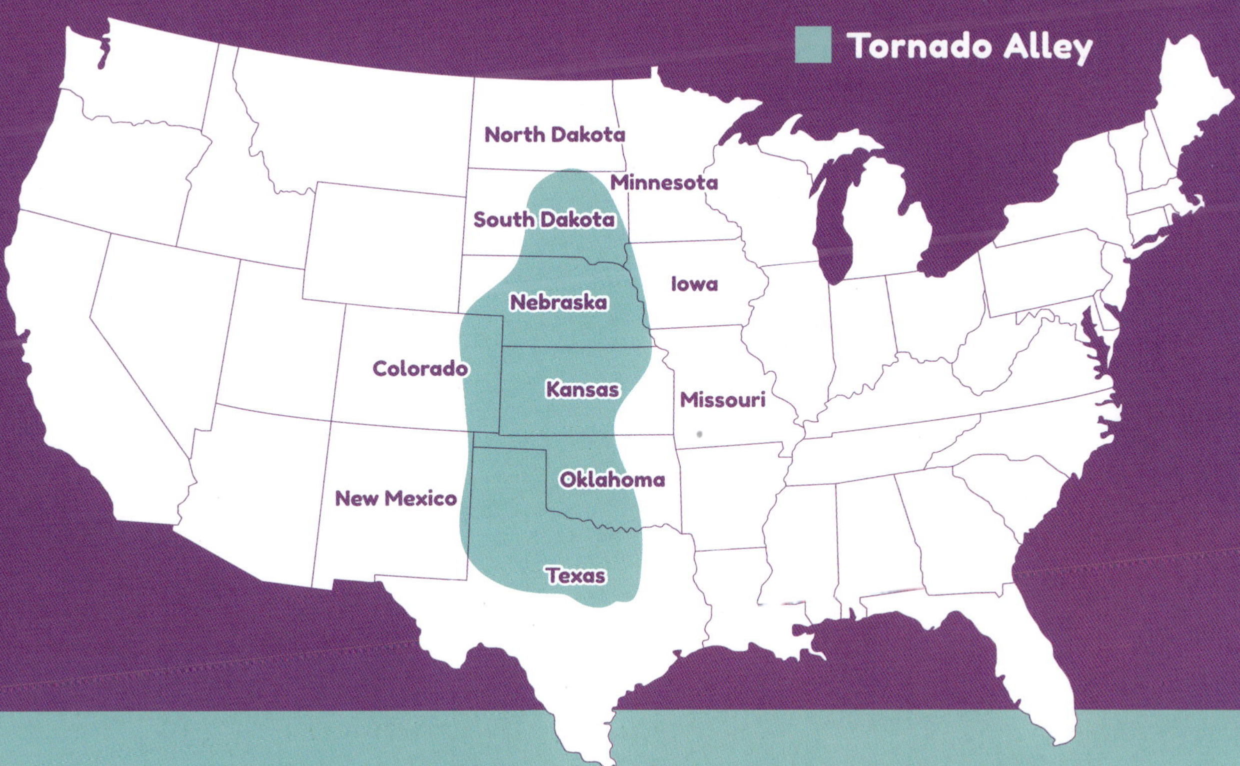

Predicting Tornadoes

Meteorologists are people who study weather. They do not always know when a thunderstorm will form a tornado. However, there are signs a tornado might be coming.

Researchers use Doppler radar to study tornadoes. This type of radar tracks velocity of objects, which is speed and direction together.

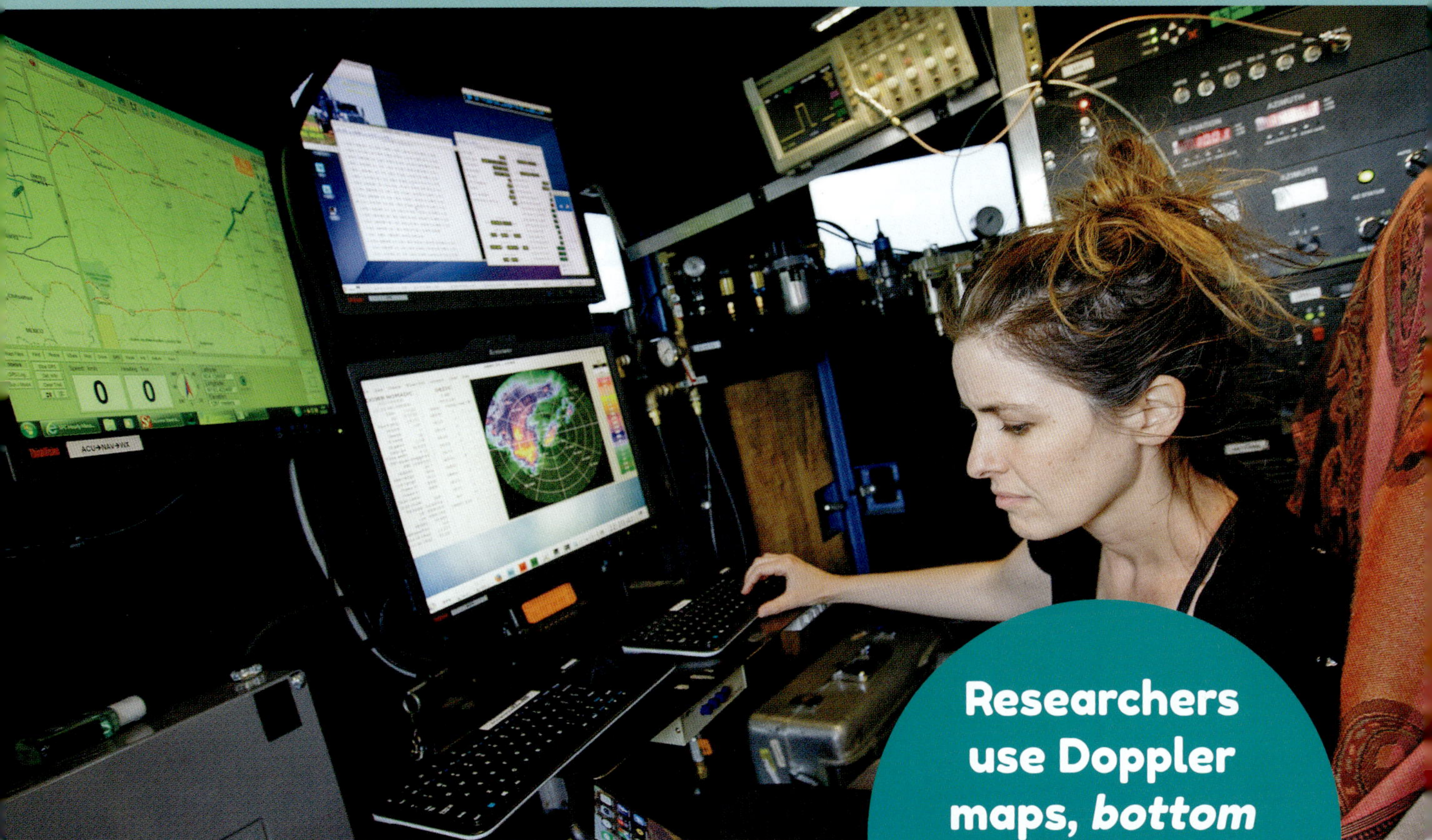

Researchers use Doppler maps, ***bottom screen***, to look for signs of tornadoes.

Signs

Before a tornado, the sky might be very dark. It might turn a strange color such as brown, green, or yellow. There could be a sound like the loud roar of a train. A funnel or cone shape may start to show in the sky. Or there might be debris in the wind. This is a sign of very strong wind.

Tornadoes can be more than one mile (1.6 km) wide.

Measuring Tornadoes

Meteorologists use the Enhanced Fujita (EF) Scale to measure tornadoes. The scale goes from 0 to 5. It measures the speed of the winds in the tornado. It also measures how much damage a tornado can do.

Scale Range

An EF-0 tornado has winds at least 65 miles per hour (105 kmh). An EF-5 tornado has winds more than 200 miles per hour (322 kmh).

Tornadoes that happen over water are called waterspouts.

Effects of Tornadoes

Many tornadoes are weak. They disappear quickly. But strong tornadoes can destroy many things. The wind from tornadoes can rip through trees and buildings. It also lifts things from the ground.

Tornadoes can lift and flip vehicles.

People without basements can go to a storm shelter if a tornado is nearby.

Lifting Objects

A tornado with very fast winds can lift objects as heavy as cars. Then the wind may fling them through the air. Flying objects are one of the biggest dangers of tornadoes.

Tornado Safety

If a tornado comes near a home, people should go to a basement or small ground-floor room. They should stay away from windows. They should cover their heads and bodies.

Severe droughts can cause streams to dry up.

What Is a Drought?

A drought happens when a place gets less rain or snow than usual for a long period of time. Droughts can happen anywhere. Deserts are usually dry. That does not mean they are always in a drought. But if a rainforest got as little water as a desert for a year, it would have a drought.

Length

Droughts can last for a few weeks. They can also go on for years. Several conditions cause droughts.

Drought Map

Maps can show how long areas have been in drought, with red being the longest.

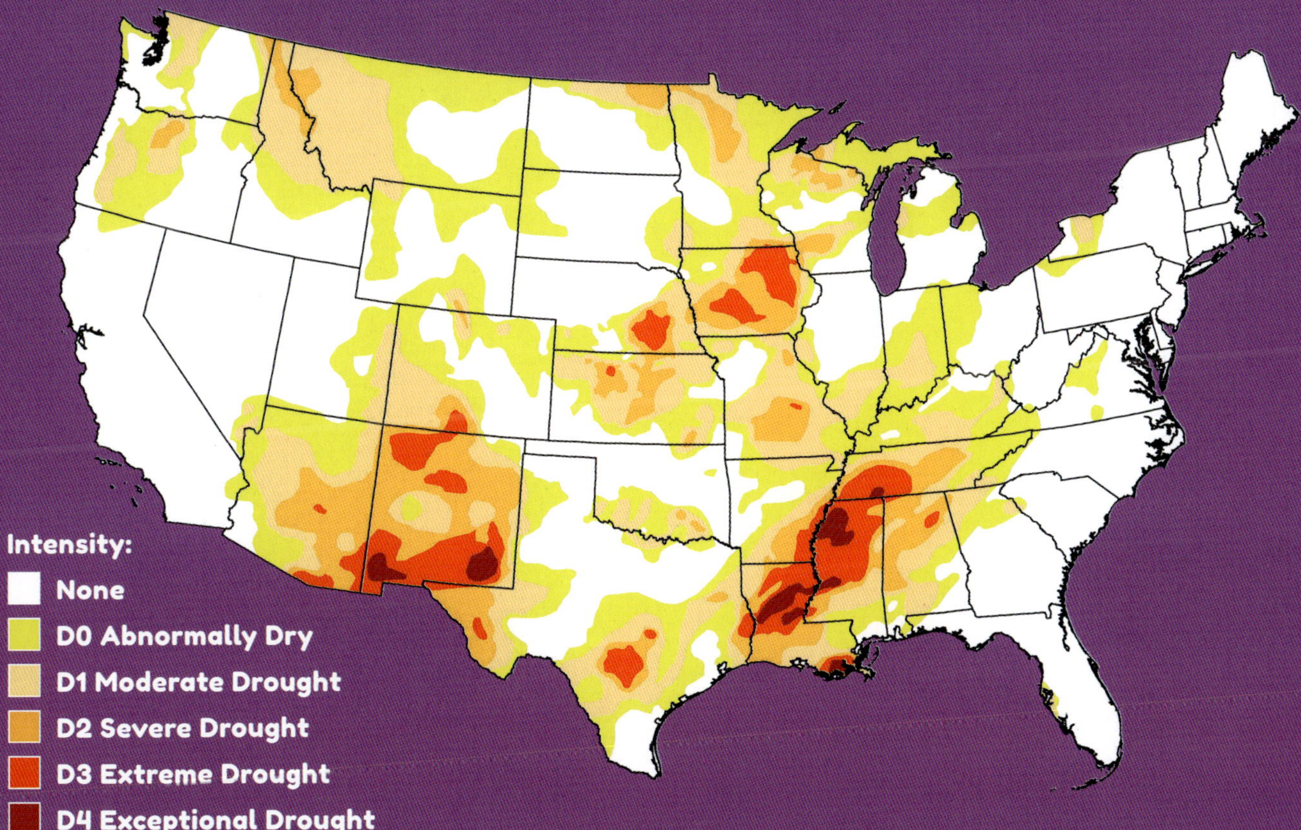

Causes of Droughts

Droughts happen when the water cycle changes. For example, a weather pattern called El Niño happens every few years. Water in a part of the Pacific Ocean gets warmer. This warmer weather can cause storms to form in unexpected places. Some parts of the world get more rain than usual. Others get less.

Human Causes

Humans can also cause droughts. People need a lot of water to drink and to

Droughts can cause bodies of water to shrink. Docks may no longer reach the water.

People can help save water by only using what they need.

water crops. People also need water for showers and toilets. Cities, towns, and farms get this water from nature. Using too much can cause droughts.

Researchers measure the depth of bodies of water to track droughts.

Measuring Droughts

Scientists use indicators to see how serious a drought is. One indicator is how much water is in the soil. Another is the amount of water in bodies of water such as streams.

Drought Index

A drought index uses indicators to assign a drought a number. That number is part of a range that rates the drought's severity. The Palmer Drought Severity Index is a common drought measurement.

Palmer Drought Severity Index

The Palmer Drought Severity Index uses a series of colors to indicate on a map which regions are driest and which are wettest.

DRY CONDITIONS

Driest | **Least Dry**

WET CONDITIONS

Least Wet | **Wettest**

Effects of Droughts

Humans, plants, and animals all need water. A long drought can make it hard for living things to survive. Droughts can kill crops. This can cause food shortages.

Dust Bowl

The Dust Bowl was one of the worst droughts in US history. It happened in the 1930s. It was named for the dust storms it caused.

When plants do not get enough water, they wilt and eventually die.

Fire can spread quickly in an area with dry grasses.

Causing Fires

Droughts make fires more likely. Dry material catches fire more easily than wet material. The fire can spread quickly.

Wildfires can burn large areas of land.

What Is a Wildfire?

A fire is a chemical reaction. It happens when a fuel combines with oxygen and heat. Oxygen is an element in the air. When some fuels meet oxygen and heat, they burn. This reaction causes heat and light. It also forms carbon dioxide and water vapor. The burning process can also make smoke.

Fuel

Many things in nature can be fuel for fires. Trees and grasses can catch fire easily. Wildfires happen when a fire spreads in nature or cropland. Wildfires are not controlled by humans.

FUN FACT!

Firefighters sometimes set small, planned fires. This controlled burning of dry material helps prevent bigger fires.

Dry wood can burn and spread fire.

Types of Wildfires

There are a few types of wildfires. Ground fires burn material such as roots underground. They also burn the duff layer. This is the layer of dead material from plants, such as fallen leaves. Ground fires spread slowly.

Ground fire

Surface and Crown Fires

Surface fires burn things close to the ground. These can be short plants, such as shrubs and grasses. Crown fires burn the upper parts of trees, such as branches. Surface fires often spread to the crowns of trees. In fact, many wildfires are a combination of ground, surface, and crown fires.

People should not leave a campfire until the coals are no longer smoldering and are cool enough to touch. Otherwise the fire could flare up again.

Causes

People sometimes cause wildfires. Campers build campfires. If they don't put out those fires correctly, the campfires can become wildfires. Lightning can also start wildfires.

Wildfire Stats

In 2023, there were about 55,000 wildfires in the United States. People caused about 85 percent of them.

Stopping Wildfires

Wildfires can be small. They may burn out on their own. Rainfall can sometimes stop or slow a wildfire.

Wind pushes wildfires across a landscape.

Big Wildfires

Sometimes wildfires spread over large areas. California gets more wildfires than any other US state. These fires are most common in spring through fall. The dry, windy weather helps fire spread more easily.

Firefighters work hard to try to put out wildfires.

US Wildfires

The number of wildfires in the United States has gone down in the past decades. However, the number of square miles burned from 2004–2013 and 2014–2023 was much more than the number of square miles burned from 1994–2003.

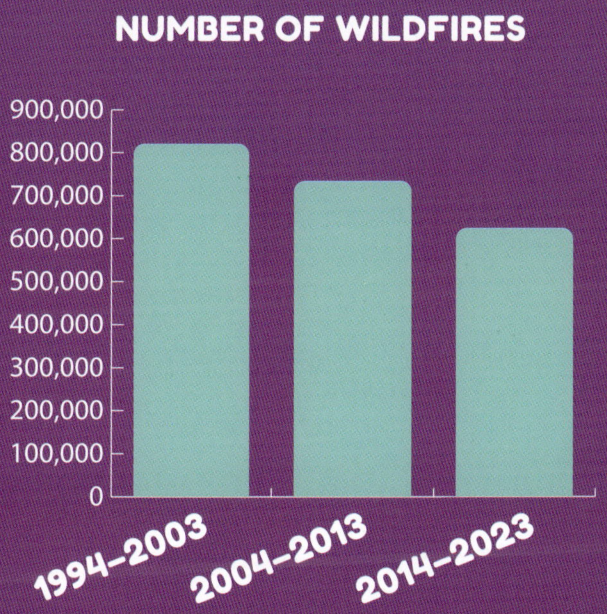

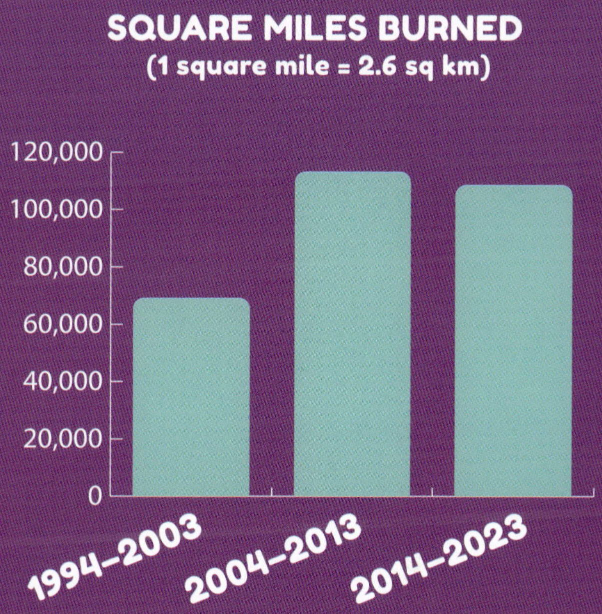

2020 Wildfires

In 2020, California had many big wildfires. These fires burned more than 6,700 square miles (17,400 sq km). That is an area bigger than the state of Connecticut.

Between 2010 and 2020, 3.4 homes were destroyed for every 4 square miles (10 sq km) of land burned by wildfires.

Effects of Wildfires

Fires are dangerous for property and people. Even people far away from fires can suffer. The smoke from wildfires spreads and pollutes the air. It has particles that are unhealthy to breathe.

Hurting Nature

Wildfires can damage nature. After fires, soil does not take in water as well. It holds less water for future growth.

Wildfires can kill large stretches of plants, destroying habitats for animals.

What Is a Dust Storm?

Dust storms happen when the wind blows dust and debris. Tiny dust particles settle on surfaces. The particles can be made of many things. They can be small bits of soil or minerals. Dust can also be plant pollen.

There is often little to no warning before a dust storm happens.

Spreading

Dust particles are small and light. A strong wind can pick them up from the ground. Dust storms happen when a strong wind carries dust with it. Often, the strong wind comes from a thunderstorm.

DUST STORMS

Texas is one state that can get dust storms.

Size

Dust storms can be very big. They can be thousands of feet high. They can stretch for many miles.

Dust Devil

Sometimes, heat from the ground makes a whirlwind of air. This whirlwind draws dust upward in a swirl. This is called a dust devil.

Sandstorms

There are different types of dust storms. A sandstorm is a very strong type of dust storm. It is strong enough to pick up and carry large particles such as sand.

Sand is bigger than dust, so it takes stronger winds to move sand.

Haboobs

The word *haboob* comes from the Arabic language. The term refers to a strong wind in Africa's Sahara Desert that makes powerful sandstorms. Today, it can also mean a quick, intense dust storm.

Haboobs sometimes hit Phoenix, Arizona.

Dust storms happen more often in deserts than other areas because there are fewer plants protecting the dusty ground.

Where Dust Storms Happen

Dust storms happen most in places with loose, dry soil. Deserts in Africa, China, and the Middle East have the most dust. This is where dust storms are common. In the United States, dust storms happen most often in the Southwest.

FUN FACT!

Earth is not the only planet with dust storms. They are also common on Mars.

Dust storms can cause low visibility.

Effects of Dust Storms

Dust storms can make it hard to travel. When dust fills the air, it is difficult to see. Very small dust particles can get inside the lungs and body. They can cause illness when breathed in. Larger pieces of dust can damage skin and eyes.

Infections

Dust can carry bacteria. When it enters the body, it can cause infections. Infections such as dust pneumonia are more common in places with dust storms.

People can cover their mouths, noses, and eyes to protect themselves from dust storms.

What Is a Heat Wave?

Some parts of Earth are naturally hotter than others. Other parts are cold in some seasons and hot in others. Heat waves happen when a place is much hotter than normal.

Air quality often becomes poor during heat waves because the air is not moving around much.

High temperatures can stress or kill crops.

Timing

Heat waves last for at least two days. Some scientists say heat waves are at least four days long. Those four days must have higher than normal temperatures. They must be temperatures that would happen only once every ten years for four days in a row.

At 95 percent humidity, 90 degrees Fahrenheit (32°C) is very likely to cause heatstroke in people. At 40 percent humidity, that same risk would happen at 108 degrees Fahrenheit (42°C).

Dry and Humid

Heat waves can be dry or humid. Humid air feels hotter than dry air. This is because people lose heat when sweat evaporates. But sweat does not evaporate as well in humid air.

The Beginning of a Heat Wave

Air currents can cause heat waves. Jet streams are currents of air that travel around the world. They are high-pressure systems. A high-pressure system is an area in the atmosphere where air is pushing away from the center.

The path of a jet stream can be shown using red to indicate hot air and blue to represent cold air.

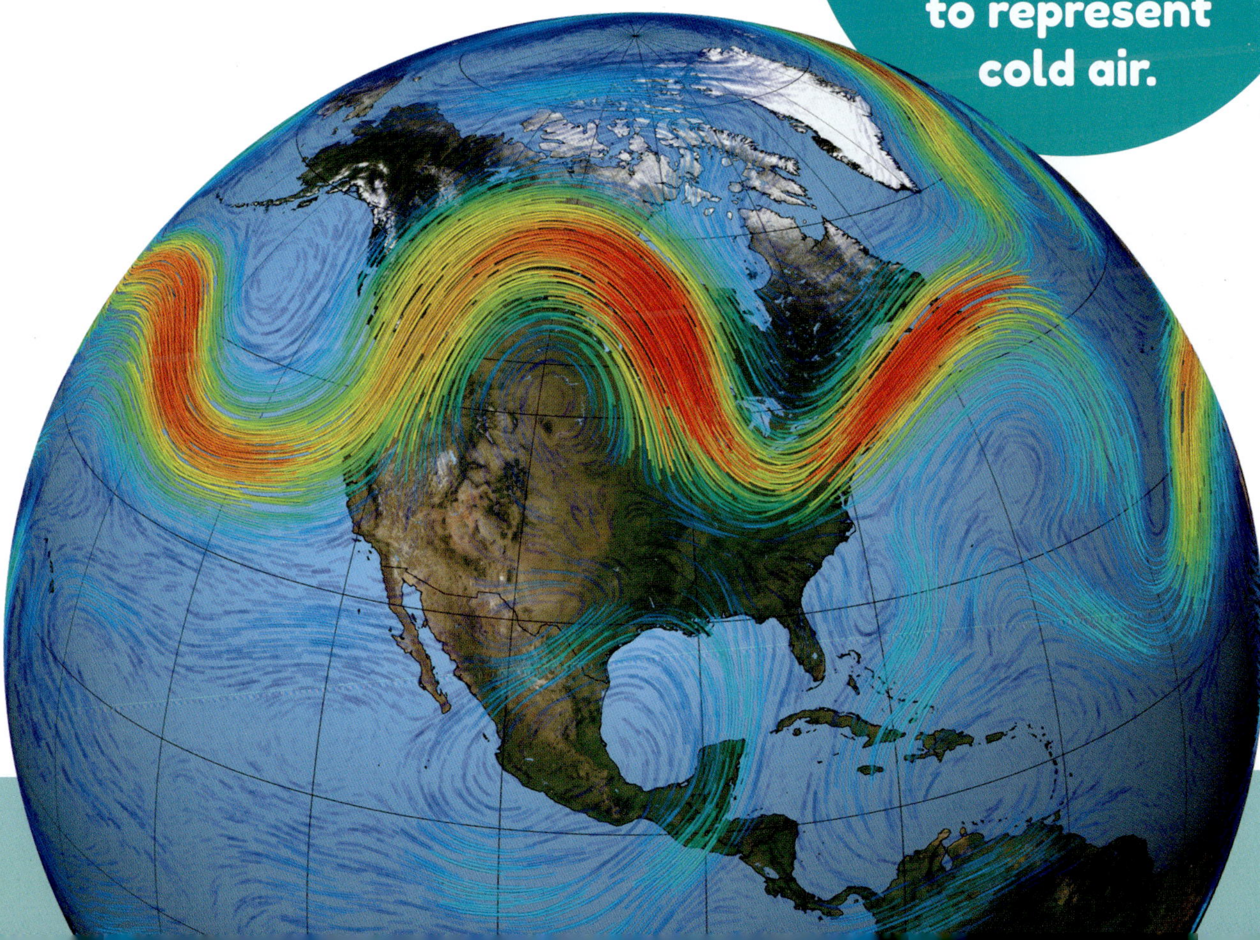

Stuck in Place

Sometimes a jet stream gets stuck. It stays in one place and pushes air downward. This warm air stays close to the surface. The jet stream also clears clouds away. The land gets more heat from the Sun.

In 2022, a satellite took an image of Paris, France, during a heat wave using a camera that detects heat. Areas with more buildings were hotter.

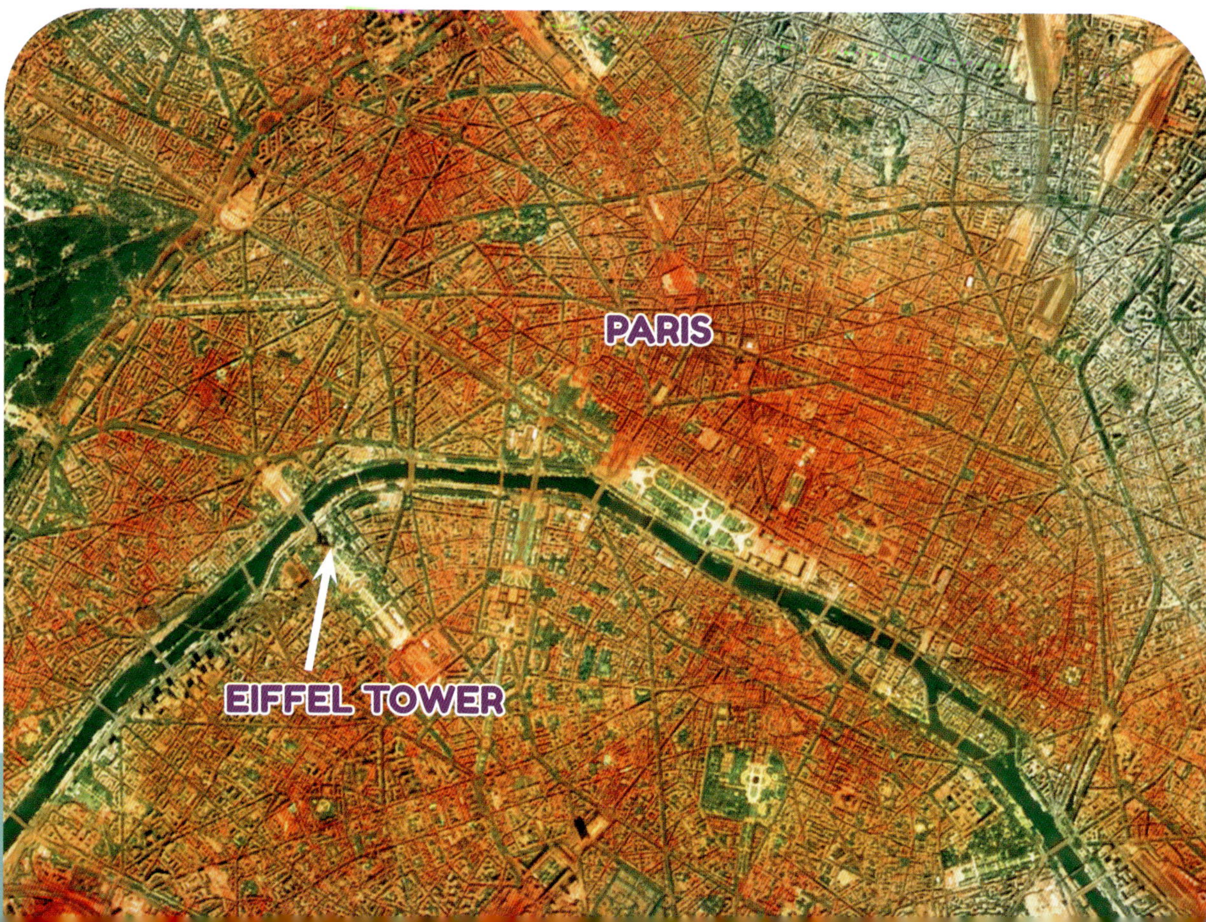

Rio de Janeiro, Brazil, had a heat wave in November 2023. People crowded at the beach to keep cool.

Where Heat Waves Happen

Heat waves are common in dry areas. They also happen in high altitudes. This is because there are more high-pressure systems there.

Power plants that burn coal are among the many sources of greenhouse gases released into the air.

What Is Climate Change?

Weather is what happens from day to day. The long-term weather of a place is its climate. The world's climate is changing due to human activity.

Humans have changed Earth's atmosphere. People burn fossil fuels such as coal and oil. These fuels release greenhouse gases into the air.

Greenhouse gases help trap heat from the Sun. Instead of going back into space, more heat stays inside the atmosphere. That means the world is getting warmer. From the late 1800s to the early 2000s, Earth's temperature has risen by about 2 degrees Fahrenheit (1.1°C).

The Future of Weather

When the planet gets warmer, weather changes. For example, a warmer world means more heat waves. Wildfires happen more often than they used to. They are also becoming bigger.

Hurricanes are getting stronger too. The ocean is warmer than it used to be. Warm water helps feed hurricanes. People are working to solve the problem of climate change. They are trying to help people live in a world with less extreme weather.

GLOSSARY

altitude
The distance above Earth's surface.

atmosphere
The gases that surround an object in space.

atom
The smallest unit of matter.

current
The regular movement of water or air in a certain direction.

debris
Fragments and remains of something.

elevation
The height above sea level.

evaporate
To turn from liquid into vapor.

index
A measure that shows the number or amount of something.

latitude
The distance north or south of the equator.

meteorologist
A scientist who studies weather.

particle
A small piece of material.

pollution
Human-made waste that harms the environment.

tropical
Relating to an area near the equator, which is the invisible line around the middle of Earth, that is warm enough for plants to grow year-round.

TO LEARN MORE

More Books to Read

Dendy, Christina. *Physical Science*. Abdo, 2025.

Farndon, John, Sean Callery, and Miranda Smith. *Weather*. Scholastic, 2020.

Water Cycles: The Source of Life from Start to Finish. DK, 2021.

Online Resources

Booklinks
NONFICTION NETWORK
FREE! ONLINE NONFICTION RESOURCES

To learn more about weather, please visit **abdobooklinks.com** or scan this QR code. These links are routinely monitored and updated to provide the most current information available.

INDEX

atmosphere, 5, 6, 8–9, 13, 21, 34–35, 38, 119, 124–125

climate change, 124–125

effects, 20–21, 27–29, 37, 44–45, 52–53, 57, 61, 69, 78–79, 88–89, 96–97, 106–107, 114–115, 122–123

measurements, 35, 36, 77, 86–87, 94–95

United States, 26, 32, 51, 74, 82–83, 96, 102, 104–105, 113

wind, 7, 12, 21, 35, 42, 70–71, 76–79, 85–89, 104, 108–109, 110, 112

PHOTO CREDITS

Cover Photos: Shutterstock Images, front (clouds, ground, black sunglasses, red sunglasses, boots), back; Tatiana Popova/Shutterstock Images, front (umbrella)

Interior Photos: Palmer Kane LLC/Shutterstock Images, 1; Red Line Editorial, 3, 31, 39, 55 (chart), 83, 95, 105; Shutterstock Images, 4, 5, 7 (bottom), 8, 9, 14 (top), 14 (bottom), 15, 17, 18, 19, 22, 23, 24, 27 (top), 28, 29, 30, 33 (top), 33 (bottom), 36 (pea), 36 (quarter), 36 (egg), 36 (softball), 37, 42, 46, 47 (top), 47 (bottom), 48, 52, 54 (top), 54 (bottom), 55 (leaf), 56, 71, 73 (bottom), 75, 76, 89 (bottom), 90, 92–93, 93, 96 (top), 96 (bottom), 97, 99, 100, 102 (bottom), 103, 107, 110 (bottom), 118, 122, 123 (top); SJ Travel Photo and Video/Shutterstock Images, 6; Klanarong Chitmung/Shutterstock Images, 7 (top); Kajeab Pongsiri/Shutterstock Images, 10; Frank Wagner/Shutterstock Images, 11; Rafal Dlugosz/Shutterstock Images, 12; Blue Ring Media/Shutterstock Images, 13; Jacques Descloitres/MODIS Land Rapid Response Team/GSFC/NASA, 16; Evgeny Atamanenko/Shutterstock Images, 20; Gina Ferazzi/Los Angeles Times/Getty Images, 21; Gritsalak Karalak/Shutterstock Images, 25; Ayman Haykal/Shutterstock Images, 26; Afanasiev Andrii/Shutterstock Images, 27 (bottom); Jim Reed Photography/Science Source, 32, 69; Marcel Paschertz/Shutterstock Images, 34; William Dudley/Shutterstock Images, 35; Barysevich Iryna/Shutterstock Images, 36 (cup); Abrosimava Tatsiana/Shutterstock Images, 36 (grapefruit); Vitalii Mamchuk/Shutterstock Images, 38; Alexey Kljatov/Shutterstock Images, 40; Jason Doiy/iStockphoto, 40–41; Evgeny Bakharev/Shutterstock Images, 43; Marcus Placidus/Shutterstock Images, 44; Allison Dinner/Bloomberg/Getty Images, 45; Songquan Deng/Shutterstock Images, 49; Nikolay Zaborskikh/Shutterstock Images, 50; Efimova Anna/Shutterstock Images, 51; Pornprasert Khanchitchai/Shutterstock Images, 53; NHPA/Photoshot/Science Source, 57; John Lee Fox/Shutterstock Images, 58; M. Volodymyr/Shutterstock Images, 59; Anna Light/Shutterstock Images, 60 (left); Natalya On/Shutterstock Images, 60 (right); Paul Maguire/Shutterstock Images, 61, Cloudsrest Images/Shutterstock Images, 62; Patryk Kosmider/Shutterstock Images, 63; Oleksandr Melnychenko/Shutterstock Images, 64; James Whitlock/Shutterstock Images, 65; Jeff Gammons/Shutterstock Images, 66; Armand Rochas/Shutterstock Images, 67; John D. Sirlin/Shutterstock Images, 68, 108; NOAA/NASA, 70; Prasanta Biswas/Majority World/Universal Images Group/Getty Images, 72; Bertha Wang/AFP/Getty Images, 73 (top); Arthur Villator/Shutterstock Images, 74; NASA Images/Shutterstock Images, 77; Terry Kelly/Shutterstock Images, 78; Felix Mizioznikov/Shutterstock Images, 79; Minerva Studio/Shutterstock Images, 80, 87; GSW Photography/Shutterstock Images, 81; Tayfun Coskun/Anadolu Agency/Getty Images, 82; Jim Reed/Science Source, 84; Drew Angerer/Getty Images News/Getty Images, 85; Limitless Production Group/Shutterstock Images, 86; Martin Haas/Shutterstock Images, 88; Larry Miller/Science Source, 89 (top); David Simeral/Western Regional Climate Center/US Department of Agriculture/NOAA/National Drought Mitigation Center at the University of Nebraska-Lincoln, 91; I. Noyan Yilmaz/Shutterstock Images, 94; Elkins Eye Visuals/Shutterstock Images, 98, 106; Colin Dewar/Shutterstock Images, 101; Yulia Nemchenko/Shutterstock Images, 102 (top); Irfan Khan/Los Angeles Times/Getty Images, 104; Jacques Descloitres/MODIS Rapid Response Team/GSFC/NASA, 109; Caleb Holder/Shutterstock Images, 110 (top); Yerbolat Shadrakhov/Shutterstock Images, 111; Ross D. Franklin/AP Images, 112; Stanley Dullea/Shutterstock Images, 113; Eli Hartman/Odessa American/AP Images, 114; Ding Genhou/Visual China Group/Getty Images, 115; Eli Mordechai/Shutterstock Images, 116; J. J. Gouin/Shutterstock Images, 117; Trent L. Schindler/Goddard Space Flight Center Scientific Visualization Studio/NASA, 119; NASA/JPL/Science Source, 120; Buda Mendes/Getty Images News/Getty Images, 121; Sercan Kucuksahin/Anadolu Agency/Getty Images, 123 (bottom); Joseph Sohm/Visions of America/Universal Images Group/Getty Images, 124